AF515729

MAHABHARATA STORIES

The City of Indraprastha

Subhadra Sen Gupta

Om Books International

The elders of the family–Bhishma, Dhritarashtra and Vidura–welcomed the Pandava brothers along with Kunti and Draupadi to Hastinapur. Bhishma was very happy that they were all alive, but Dhritarashtra was not.

Bhishma said to the Pandavas, "I feel that the kingdom should be divided into two. As Dhritarashtra is ruling over Hastinapur, it is better if Yudhishthira is crowned as the king of a new kingdom."

A new kingdom with Indraprastha as its capital was given to the Pandavas. However, neither the Kauravas nor the Pandavas were happy with their new kingdoms. Duryodhana was unhappy at losing half the kingdom and Bhima felt that their new kingdom was too small.

Meanwhile, after travelling with Krishna to the kingdom of Dwarka Arjuna met Krishna's sister Subhadra and fell in love with her. When the elders of the family did not agree to the marriage, he eloped with Subhadra. However, Krishna stepped in and spoke up for them and got Arjuna and Subhadra married.

Subhadra was welcomed in Indraprastha with great fanfare and Krishna became the adviser to the new king, Yudhishthira. He suggested to Yudhishthira to build a new capital with many palaces and then to hold the Rajasuya Yagya.

The Rajasuya Yagya is a fire ritual during which a powerful king invites other kings who come and pay him respect and offer tributes. Krishna knew that with the yagya Yudhishthira would be respected as a powerful king.

Yudhishthira summoned the danava, Maya, who was the architect of the asuras and ordered him to build a grand palace for the Pandavas. Arjuna said to Maya, "Build us a palace that no one on earth has seen before."

Soon Maya showed them around the new palace. It was built of marble and precious stones were set into the walls and pillars. It was also full of illusory things like a sparkling floor that looked like a pool of water.

Maya showed the Pandavas a room where the floor looked like solid marble when it was really a pool of water.

Maya said, “In my illusory palace you have to be very careful while you walk, Your Majesty. Here you could fall into a pool and get wet!”

The day of the Rajasuya Yagya arrived. The palace built by Maya looked magnificent as all the kings of the land came to Indraprastha and bowed before Yudhishthira.

The Kauravas wandered around the palace and were full of admiration and envy at the achievement of the Pandavas. Dusshasana said to Duryodhana, “Brother, our palace is like a hut compared to this heavenly palace.”

Duryodhana saw the room where the floor sparkled like a lotus pool and thinking it to be water, refused to step on it. Arjuna walked across with a laugh, “Ah, Brother Duryodhana! This is marble, not water. You have been fooled!”

Next day, Duryodhana entered the room which was, in fact, a pool but was tricked into thinking it to be a floor made of marble, he stepped on it and fell into water. Draupadi saw him and began to laugh at the sight of a very wet Duryodhana.

An angry Duryodhana called his brothers and Shakuni and said, "The Pandavas invited us here only to insult us. Let us leave immediately!"

Duryodhana plotted, "Dusshasana, I cannot bear to see the Pandavas become so rich and powerful. We have to take away Indraprastha from them."

Dusshasana suggested, "Let us ask Uncle Shakuni to find a way to make them lose their kingdom."